A Cup of Inspiration To Go Please

My Heart Runneth Over

Holly Coop

A Cup of Inspiration To Go Please
My Heart Runneth Over

A Cup of Inspiration To Go Please
My Heart Runneth Over

© 2016 Holly Coop

ISBN: 9798991103206
ISBN-13: 9798991103206

All Rights Reserved

No part of this book in any way may be used or reproduced in any manner whatsoever without written permission except in the case of brief quotations embodied in critical articles or reviews.

Cover Art Credit:
 with permission of Artist (unnamed)

Other publications from Author

Heart Strings - Forever Wanderer

Locks of Love – A Book of Encouragement

A Line in the Sand –
A Journey Towards Forgiveness

DEDICATION

This book is dedicated to all the wonderful people who bless my life everyday. Their warm, loving, and generous hearts are the reason – *My heart runneth over* - and I thank God for you.

Contents

Various inspirational poems and quotes from my heart to yours.

Portrait of a Mother

Her shoulders carry the burdens
Her smile silently defends
Creases show a mind filled with worry
On a face etched with the pain
She has endured
Yet a generous spirit pours out
from a heart remaining pure
And though she feels
like dropping to the ground
She stands
and continues to carry on

The love of a Mother is profound
Her portraits frame - *a crown*

Hugs

I like to have the last hug
So, it lasts
long

I like long hugs
They fill my heart
with song

I like hugs from you
Embrace
warmth tenderly strong

I like hugs
as the day is long

Far-Sighted

Sometimes, you have to look closely –
to see a heart
But it is there

When a Heart Escapes – Joy Fades

If you are not present with your heart
Another may slip away
Let your love know
They are the gift that fills your day

Thank You for This Autumn Day

Thank You for This Day

For the sun that will soon rise
to bring us warmth and light
For its partner Earth,
graciously provides
the resources of life
For the people - family – friends –
strangers, we will meet who bring us joy
For our jobs, our schools,
our blessings to volunteer
And all the blessed activities
each day that we hold dear –

They keep us connected
motivated
learned
sharing
busy to enjoy the day given
Where Karma rounds its turn

Thank you for the opportunities
To work - To play - To Love
To achieve - To wake
To rest - To sleep
To fall and rise above
To Just BE
To see - To touch
To hear - To breath
and thank you
For the magnificent view looking upward
of beautifully colored leaves

Constraints

Free Bird
I give you freedom
Under certain terms of use

I will be the one to say
What you can and cannot do

Your will is free to be abused
By nearly everyone – but you

I take your common good to heart
I'll wave you to the finish line
Provided I allow you to start

I am the all-knowing government
I can see and do you harm

My strong right arm will hold you
While my left gently keeps you down

Welcome to the new America
Land of the free, the brave, the proud

From metal chains binding
Bend knee and kiss my crown

Bars of cold steel will shelter you
while you wait
There is only one rule
before entering through my gate
Accept, with your free will
constraint

By Invitation Only

The universe has sent out signs.
We heed their message.
Their truths we won't deny.
The fate – it lies within the grasp
Provided it's our time.

Master Passenger

In case you are feeling unclear as to where your
life is heading
KNOW that something much bigger
is lovingly navigating your journey.
Travel it at ease
Remember to enjoy the ride
while letting The Master drive.

Worry–Free?

Let worries abate
If necessary -
acknowledge them another day
For those that have bearing -
when you're feeling less weary
You may give them a nod or two
Being careful not to be fooled
Worry is rarely beneficial to you
Let time carry your burdens
it has a knack for working things out
And freeing up energy for you
to joyfully move about
Worry
It's not free
Its cost will rob you of your peace

Enjoy

Close your eyes
Clear your mind
Let the noise of the world around you cease
Tap into the joy of inner peace
Let burdens of day
Be lifted away
Allow your worries to fade
Give them to another day
If you so choose
Refuse
Anyone to rain on your parade
Permit only those bearing smiles on face
To enter into your space
The time to enjoy
Is today

Simple Joy

Roads traveled
busy
Everybody has someplace to go
In the distance, a bird flies high
Destination
anywhere the winds blow

On a residential street
Homes lined neat
Sit empty
No faces to greet

In a vacant park near
It would appear
The only living creature in sight
A bird nestling in a tree
Resting from flight

Chattering noise fills the air,
Where mall shoppers flock

Just outside, a bird chirps happily
Prompting his feathered friends to mock
Some experience nature through its many sights and sounds
While others remain unaware of the beauty that surrounds

In the simple joys of life, much is gifted,
to those open to receive
But many keep life too busy for living to be achieved
Imagine the birds of the air,
existing without care
How much better might we humans fare?

Perfectly *Imperfect*

Toss away your perfectionistic tendencies
The universe was born from imperfection
Random bursts of energy brought forth by the
One
Who chose it to be
A well-choreographed symphony
Of stars, planets, atmosphere, and sea.
With living creatures tossed in the mix
to create a masterpiece.
A perfect plan emerges from a seemingly
imperfect mess
and so, it is with you and I
Where perfection is about as far out of reach
for us as is, the stars in the sky.
We are not to be perfect in the perfect plan
We are only to trust and submit
our imperfect natures
To the One Perfect, I AM

Imperfectly Perfect

Hey – everyone makes mistakes
Nobody is perfect
It doesn't mean you are less
It does not define your condition of heart
It is but an opportunity - new
For imperfectly perfect - YOU
To make a fresh start
One door closes
Allowing for another opened
Don't be afraid
to walk through

Minute by Minute

All is well – at the moment
I'm living one second at a time
Enjoying day by day
Loving every minute of it –
and those I meet along my way
And for each new one, I awake
Giving thanks

Good People are -

Hard to find!
So, when you find one –
Hold on tight!
Don't let a blessing - slip out of your life.

Time

We are all given it
Some waste it - Some use it wisely
Some keep it to themselves –
Some share it kindly

Time

All having a precise number of days
For each, it is not the same
The choice is individually ours
How we fill our years, days, and hours
How can we keep - *time* from gaining speed?
Leave our lost time - in the past
Stop our future from moving too fast
Make our present moments last
By enjoying this *time* that we have

Time

Too Much Time on My

Time - something in the distant past –
slips away from us so fast
Looking ahead, we plan to grasp –
but with its speed, we are unable to catch
In our busyness
there is no such thing as having time
There is only, making time
Do it before yours runs out
Spend some - with those you love
That is what this life - is about

Do It Afraid!

Change is not easy
It is so scary
Do it anyway
While you are afraid
You will be much happier
Then had, you stayed
Do it – afraid

Loud and Clear

Your heart
Is heard
Because your actions
Speak as loud as your words
A person's words and actions
Tell the true story of their heart
At times may be discouraging
But the truth – it must be known
A person's words and actions
It's how their true heart - is shown

Where I Lead – Will You Follow?

When hearts lead –
Follow with speed

Life Recipe

Strong Body
Balanced Mind
Happy Heart

Middle Ground

No more up-and-down emotional extremes
Comfortably coasting in the middle
is a pleasant place to be
Maybe I'll stay there.

CHA...CHA...Change

No matter the potential gain
It is never easy
When your familiar goes through change
Stand strong
you will get through
Remember - CHANGE
can be good for you

Finders Keepers – Losers Weepers

Whoever said it is better to have loved and lost
than never to have loved at all –
Was NOT the loser!

Nature Talks

Only when we listen are we able to see more

Your greatness
is so magnified
in the sights and sounds of nature

How small a creature am I
against the backdrop of the view

To experience this leaves me in awe
Feeling closer to Your goodness –
than I have ever felt before

When Nature Talks
I long to hear more

Vacation Time Recipe

Arrive early
Leave late
Savor a slow simmer in between
Will serve to satisfy –
With a bit of craving for more
Keeping you motivated for planning
your next great getaway - of explore.

A Little Birdie Told Me

Do What Makes Your Heart Leap
and soon you'll be jumping for joy!

Taking Steps

I don't want merely to wait in limbo –
for life to happen to me

I rather participate –
as it is unfolding before me

One never knows
what the universe has in store –
and one never will

Until one is willing to let the past close –
take steps towards a new open door

Busy Lives' Buzz By

We are all busy
But you should never be
too busy
For those you care about
Because some day they may not
Be there
to care

Ambitious people

It is a good thing to be
driven
As long as you are driving
 in the direction you should go
Priorities
They usually leave lots of signs on the road

The Music in Your Life

Experience the joy of the music in your life.
Savor the melody you are playing,
Enjoy the rhythm of your day

Some moments will be in harmony –
some - a little out of tune
But as a whole, it is an orchestra
However, your ensemble comes into form –
When it all blends
a symphony is born

Some days are upbeat –
others drag along - like a low baritone
Whatever may be the tune of the day -
relax and make it your own.

Experience the joy of the music in your life
Savor the melody you are playing
Enjoy the rhythm of your day
We are only given a short time, to play

Thrifty or Just Cheap

Spending money and making money
Focused on material things
Leaves a pocketbook empty
And a heart forever in need
vs
Spending money on moments
And earning riches in loving relationships –
Equals
Time well spent

Put your money where your heart is.
Share the gift of life with others
who hold values like your own
Those are the kinds of people
 you want to get to know
The happiness and joy you will find
will be
priceless

Seasons of the Soul

Ever-changing are we
From a past where we have come
To a moment, we now see
In movement to a future where
Our best is yet to be

Night and Day

Only in your darkness
can you fully see His Light

Swimming Lessons

Lord – Push me out of my boat
into Your deep waters
and teach me how to swim.

Sky High

When the sky is the limit
To succeed –
you cannot be afraid of heights

Good Morning, TODAY

Thank You for the day
Let me live in each of its moments
With no expectations for it
Good or bad - Happy or sad
Dry eyes or wet - No worries - No regrets
It is after all
A Day!

Not like the ones that have passed
Except that it will be gone
just as fast
There are no guarantees – for you or me
That another will come our way
So, let us accept
The gift that is NOW
By enjoying this time called TODAY

Use up every second of it –
By being the best YOU – you can be

Pass on kind words and love
Give free smiles and hugs

Remember a gift
is meant to be shared
If we are lucky enough for a tomorrow to come
We may find that yesterday
was the last today - for some
And for others –
a missed opportunity – to love

Be Alert

Love rarely hears
what the mind is speaking
and only listens to what is beating
in its heart.

Walk the Talk

Be careful while on your journey
that your open mind
doesn't lead you down the path
of narrow thinking

I Ponder

Since the past does not exist at all
In the minute blip of time in which it occurs
it is gone
Then why do we insist on letting it
in our minds - live on?
Why do we let something
non-existent
wreak such havoc in our lives
by allowing it to be a memory
that continues on and on?
Let it go –
the universe did a long time ago.

Que Sera Sera - *or something like that*

I am not in charge of destiny
Fate is not my forte
I can only hope to remain open
For the opportunities, God chooses
To allow into my day
What is – IS
Whatever is to be
WILL BE
The Universe
doesn't require anything –
Except perhaps an open heart –
from me

Thank You

Thank you, Lord, for this day
Fill me with Your wisdom
that will guide me toward Your way

Not keeping me from stumbling
but lifting me from my fall
Show me Your great mercy
when my flesh ignores Your call

Walking with me
through the uncertainties
that this world throws in my path
Teaching me to navigate
to boldly walk right past

Let my eyes see clearly
Your light that shines beyond
Nudge me just a little
with Your whisper
Stay calm and carry on

Precious Moments

Chores will always be there -
no matter how long you wait
The chances of someone
sneaking in and doing them for you
are slim, I would say
And if it were to happen -
now, wouldn't that be GREAT!

As for the people you love –
on the other hand –
it is not the same, I'm afraid
We never know if we will live –
to see them another day

In and out of our world they go –
someday may be the last
Keeping that in mind – I'll choose
To spend as many precious moments with them
as I possibly can

Star Light Star Bright
Make My Wish Come True Tonight

For every star, my eyes do see
Is the coming true of another's dream
Every star in the night's bright sky
Is another wish coming true

And in my wildest dreams, I never
Wished for anyone but you

As its brightening light shines high
The heart of faith can conclude
That surely
Those bright lights in the sky
Are dreams all coming true

Body Beautiful

Love your body
no matter its shape or size
For it is the place
Your beautiful spirit
resides

Isn't it a bit – Ironic?

In our quest for Happiness
we have become increasingly unhappy.

Hug Happy Today!

It is unfortunate that for many –
Happy is not detected
until it becomes a memory passed.

And often, it is brought to mind
as a means by which to cope –
when we are visited by the always uninvited
and most times unannounced – sad

Hug Happy Today –
it often shows up in unexpected ways
and sometimes does not last.

Early Bird

With much of life being sad –
All the more reason to embrace HAPPY –
Whenever it chooses to flutter into our path.

I had the honor of hearing this morning –
the early bird catching his worm

In the wee early hours of the morning
When I pull myself from the slumber of my bed
A rush of cheerful sounds fills my groggy head

My eyes brighten wide
And my sleepy ears perk
By the orchestra
of lively chirping birds

Cool, night breezes slip in through windows
not shut tight
Allowing for the enjoyment of this slice
of spring delight

Oh, the freedom of springtime
Surely felt by all
No matter if you fly the skies of this earth
Or walk on two legs
proud and tall

Creation all around us -
sings its joyful song

I wish it could be springtime all year long.

Tread Carefully –
You are on POSITIVE Ground

A good rule of thumb –
to keep your foot away from your tongue

With every complaint that falls from your lips
A blessing should surely follow –
Because a constant negative tone
is hard
for a confident heart to wallow
Allow goodness to flow from your words
that flood those around you
Show others the well of your heart runs deep
by not conforming to what is shallow –
Keep your feet from getting too wet
in the pity pool, they tend to like to wallow
Remember - frowning quickens wrinkles
While smiling produces none
Being one or around - a negative Nellie -
is never any fun

Acceptance without Question

You have to accept people for who they are
Not for what they are to you

Sometimes, we build people up to hold an
importance in our lives –
which we perceive we cannot live without
Don't expect others to be something for you
that you feel is lacking within
You will end up being disappointed every time
and it is not even fair to them

Be what you need to be for you
Embrace every person and experience
that comes into and exits your life -
Know that they were meant to be,
in that moment of time

Often only felt – and seen with blind eyes
For reasons known or unknown
It is not always for us to decide

Whether something exists as temporary
or for life
What will be, will be – it is not always precise
Appreciate those present in your life
and the blessings they are – or were
Nothing in the universe
is for you to know for sure

In a single lifetime, the opening and closing of
doors – may be many
I only need to have faith and know
fate will guide me
Stop trying to figure out what your destiny is –
just trust that it will be
Life - is not meant to be taken
quite so seriously

What's Black and White and – *Gray?*

Stop looking at everything in your life
As only black or white
There is an awful lot of gray
On an ordinary day
Clear the path for an open mind
You may be surprised
From what you can find
Lose the preconceptions
That only serves to keep you blind
Happy is attainable – when given a little time

A Chill in the Air

I love the season of fall
But hate to see summer go
It is just too early
For the air to be this cold
Your season will arrive soon enough
So why not give us more time
of sun
I love the season of fall
But hate to see the warmth
of summer days – be gone

Do The Math

Start counting blessings
Stop adding up complaints
You will find multiplying in your life
An abundance of joy-filled days
To sum it up –
It all equals out in the end, anyway

How's the Reception?
Is my reaction coming in loud and clear?

When pushed too far
I tend to be a reactor rather than a receptor.
Don't push buttons
unless you are willing to take - the jolt

Have's and Have Not's – Which Have You Got?

Stop wishing for all your
have-nots
and start rejoicing in all your
have's
Soon, your heart will cease
to be saddled with sappy
Your mood will increase
with happy
Your entire life will burst free
with an exuberant feeling
of GLAD

Don't Get Hooked on the Perfectness

For perfect, there is no such thing
It only keeps you from doing in life
Limiting your ability to succeed

To set your mind on this notion –
is to start every morning with a fumble
Setting you up every day of your life - to stumble

In essence, your life CAN be perfect
Just simply by being not
When you finally realize this, you begin to see –
what a perfectly-perfect life
you have got

Speak My Language, *or say nothing at all*

Sarcasm – the language of cowards,
a mask - true feelings can hide behind
Sarcasm is nothing more than a disguise
Keeping from the outside world
what a heart holds inside
Sarcasm speaks the truth if you can read
between the lines
But a person of courage is unafraid
of speaking the truth
You know what they mean
without being a feelings sleuth
They wear their feelings proudly
and some right on their sleeve
You will never wonder by the words they speak –
what their words truly mean
Speak a language that is true to your heart
Let the sarcasm from your lips – depart

Give Me a PEACE of Your Mind

Jaws keep flapping while words keep spilling out
But not a one is comprehended
when all I hear are
SHOUTS!
People keep talking - But few stop to think
What is about to tumble off their lips
before they speak
My ears seldom listen
when your decibel is at its peak
A voice at a softer volume
will get more attention from me

To Be or Not to Be – Human

Smiling faces rather than glares
Words that encourage replacing insults blared
Helping hands willing to lend
Hearts open to loving one another
People with ideals that are not afraid to bend
Until these elements get replenished
within our society –
it saddens me to say
the moral structure of our human race –
is slowly fading away.

If we remain un-open to receive
what our hearts desperately need.
If we continue on our narrow pathways
going nowhere at fast-paced speeds
If we make our decisions
not rooted in integrity
but rather stemming from greed
If we continue destroying each other

in the name of religion – of war and of choices
appearing free
We will soon be extinguished - from our reality

Left behind will be fragments of a people who
once knew love.
Now empty shells – not a soul
just flesh and blood

The choice was our free will
But free we cannot be
Without the presence of God
We have lost our humanity

What's Your Point, *of view?*

Sitting in the drive-through at the bank
I noticed something up in the sky.
I said to my daughter sitting beside me
on the passenger's side –
"Look at that up there."
From the position of the drive-through canopy
and her position in the car –
her capacity to see was not the same as mine –
thus, she replied –
" I cannot see from my point of view."

"I cannot see from my point of view."
That one seemingly insignificant sentence she spoke,
struck me quite profoundly.
How many times during our lifetime and in our relationships
are we unable to see simply because of our points of view?

Perhaps we should all sit on the driver's side
now and then
before we pass judgments – before we make
assumptions.
It is possible if we reposition ourselves a little,
we could see more clearly - the whole picture.

But it is up to us to move beyond our
comfortable seats
where we tend to sit and preach –
look at things from a slightly different angle –
allowing us to see beyond our points of view.

The capacity to see another's point of view –
is only possible if I am willing - to move.

Fill Me with Your Word Today

I am emptying and opening my mind.
My mind is now empty –
its openness is as vast as the universe.
The only thing I see with my mind's eye –
is a spec of bright light -a light which is Thee

I am starting with a blank page.
Lord - be the Author of my day.
Write the steps You desire me to take.
Script the words You want me to say.
Lord - be the Author of my day.

I lay my heart open - for You, Lord
I am the blank page. My soul is Your novel.
Fill me with Your Word today.

Let's Get in Shape

If we do not make people hurt
with our words
Or to feel fear with the actions we take.
If when we see another human being –
reaching out
We do not allow our hands to pull away
Perhaps a new world will begin to take shape.

Coping

To cope is to resolve yourself to practice
the three most essential elements of life –

Which are
To Hope
To Pray
and
To Trust
In that order!

Un-raveled

When I find myself holding on
by a single thread -

You are part of the tapestry
that weaves love into my life

More or *Less*
The Good Old Days Were Best

A cobweb of emotions –
all wound tight inside your mind
No spot that you can sit and think –
when the clutter is sky-high
Why can I not get my head on straight?
Why can I not focus and concentrate?
My thoughts and feelings are all jumbled
undefined

Could it be that I may need a bit of change?
Could it be that if not, I go insane?

When my life is like running an obstacle course
and with my energy decreasing
every move I make
is forced
The more I try to accomplish –
the less I do

And with every year that passes by
the hours seem so few

Nostalgic thoughts of days gone by
wander through my frantic mind
as I wish for something more –
that is less

A simple little existence
where we all have just what we need.
And everyone is not running around
like people on speed.
No worries because the bills are paid
with a little in the bank for a rainy day
And credit card debt
is a buried thing of the past

When a weekend felt like a week –
and a year took forever to pass
When fathers worked hard
to make it to the high society of
the middle class

And mothers fed their broods quite well
on a little bit of cash

Nowadays, it is different –
most women work away from the home
Fathers are in limbo –
not knowing which way to go
Children are all spoiled
and most don't give a damn
A great majority are being fed and clothed –
by good old Uncle Sam

No longer is there ambition to fuel a fire within
Because now, if you earn money,
it is considered the deadliest sin
Just because a lazy few,
whose desire is to remain comfortably
dependent - on YOU
It sure does spoil it for all the rest

Oh, I wish I could return to the days
when more was less

Dads were proud
moms were happy
Kids felt secure
schools weren't sappy
The government knew its place
And most families could keep up the pace
Because the Jones did not live right next door

Oh, how I wish for those good old days
When having less - meant so much more

A Daily Routine

Can make or break the day

Eat Right
Exercise
Sleep
Rest
Enjoy Life at its best

Daily Routine

For the writer in me

Just as important as brushing our teeth
Styling our hair and washing our faces
Writing is something a writer
MUST do
on a regular daily basis

When we let our busy lives
take precedence over this
It is only a matter of time
before we become an emotional mess

So, each
and every
single day
after I wake from a restful night
I'll make it a point
to sit right down at the keyboard
And allow my fingers to type

So once my face is washed,
and my teeth are brushed,
and my locks are trussed
I will then let my imagination wander undressed

Unleashing worlds of thoughts
Tucked in my mind all night
A perfect start to just a typical day
for the one who loves to write

Acknowledgements

A special thank you to my mom, the most inspiring soul I know.

Thank you, Ann and Eileen, your friendship and encouragement have been nourishment to this writer's weary soul.

Thank you Sharon for the deadline!

Thank you, my BFF Crystal, for always guiding me in the *placement* of my heart.

Vernon for your technical expertise and all the help along the way - special thanks.

Authentic art grows
from the seedlings of a humbled heart

Thank you for allowing me to share with you a little bit of my heart - through art.

The following pages contain samplings from some of my other publications and a little bit about me.

From my book:
Heart Strings – Forever Wanderer

Soul Mate, Passion Mate, Come – Breathe with me, for all eternity.

  I saw a reflection of my heart – in your beautiful soul and was instantly awakened to my truth. Drawn to look more deeply at the path I'd been lost on – fate took my hand and led me right to you.

Picking Up Pieces

I fear that you will break my heart
And there are not enough pieces left
To break apart
My head is screaming run away
My heart is leaping directly in the way
Of the pierce, from your love's aim

Fire Starter

I know I am playing with fire
But the warmth keeps drawing me in
What harm is there in wishful thinking
As long as I do not
sin?
The elements are against me
I cannot win
When love's flame ignites a lonely heart
To the passion that stirs within
I know I am playing with fire
But the warmth keeps drawing me in
How can a lonely heart defend
from a burning desire so intense?
My logic whispers
stay away
While my heart screams
jump right in

In the Palm of

I feel as though I hold a lot of hearts in my hand
And that I am deserving, of none
I pray I make the right choice of whom
 I hand over my own to
Who will be the ONE?

From my book:
Locks of Love – A Book of Encouragement

Poetry to lift the spirits of those weary of heart and to ease the emotional anguish that can develop when the body and mind are suffering. Unlock the chains that bind your spirit through illness, whether your suffering is from physical pain or emotional and mental conditions. No matter what life struggle you may be experiencing, allow your spirits to rest in the hope and knowledge that your future has and forever will be locked into the great mercy, love, and promise of Your Higher Power.

Hopes Bright

Life
Stolen from us when we are feeling submerged in depression, a deadly current.
Hope
A life jacket God gives us.

When darkness grows thicker around us,
Hope is a distant brightness
just barely visible to our naked eye.
It appears to be surrounded by and covered with a veil of darkness.
It glistens but is unreachable from our grasp.
But through the delicately woven fabric of emotions, we can see its bright persistence to shine through.
As we trudge through our darkness, we frantically reach to pull away the veil, but the fog of gloom that suffocates us keeps pushing us back, further away from Hope's shining force.

A will of perseverance that is not our own pulls us through the debilitating thickness of our night. The veil lifts just enough to fill our lungs with a resuscitative gasp as if we were drowning, our lungs now emptied of their liquid death; we are finally able to breathe in the freshness of a new day.

Faith pushes, while the brightness of Hope pulls us through the darkest patches of our journey, and Grace gives us nourishment while we trudge through

Life.

A Gentle Rain of Tears

What makes a grown woman cry?
Just about anything
at any given time.

Whenever we feel weary, broken, and alone,
To wash away the heartache.
Let tears flow
To clear out the crevices where despair gets
trapped
In the darkest areas of our souls.
Like a gentle rain, our tears cleanse,
Until once again, we feel whole.

The Roads We Choose

Rough roads are never the paths we choose for ourselves.
They are simply a reality of the journey of our natural lives.
God allows these detours that lead us to the narrow path, where He awaits

From my book:
A Line in the Sand – A Journey Towards Forgiveness

For those who struggle to forgive and those who long for forgiveness.

Tunnel Vision

I had to go through the dark tunnel to get to the light.
Now that I have,
I think I will survive.

We Walk

Our journey takes us down many roads,
And many challenges show their face.
But through the thickest part of the forest,
we walk.
Our steps can be lighter with grace.
We will no doubt cross many bridges,
And some we will burn down, too.
But at the end of our darkened tunnel,
We will see a glimmer,
And in that instance, we will know,
we've been guided the whole way by You.

Be the Bulldozer - Not the Ground

Until you stop seeing yourself as a victim
You will never get anywhere in life.

You did not have it any worse
than anybody else growing up.

Or maybe you did, but,

Everyone has fallout in their life.
From which the debris is not always easy to discard.

Emotional wounds leave painful scars.

The secret to success,
is to leave all of it in the dust.

Move forward,
Plow past,

Be the person in your dream.

Issues that paralyze,
Transform them to be what propel you,

Leap into a new today.
Stop letting the past prey upon your future.

Forgive,

Forget,

Move on.

Be the bulldozer, not the ground.

About the Author

Holly Coop resides in the Midwest with her husband, children, and furry friends.

Holly enjoys writing and publishing inspirational poetry, motivational quotes, and spiritual insights. She has authored five poetry collections. Touching hearts with words has become her life purpose. She hopes her words will stir hearts and inspire others in their purpose. In addition to writing, Holly enjoys sketching, photography, and creating art featuring her poetry.

Holly invites readers to visit her blog hollycoopauthor.wordpress.com, where she shares reflections, nuggets of wisdom, and anything that comes to mind.

HollyCoopBooks.com

Thank you for all your support.
Poetry is an art form that can change hearts and minds, open new visions for our society, and change our world, one word at a time.

I'm blessed to be able to share my love of the written art of poetry with you!
~ Holly Coop

The End

www.ingramcontent.com/pod-product-compliance
Lightning Source LLC
Chambersburg PA
CBHW050335010526
44119CB00004B/152